What's Government?

Revised Edition

Nancy Harris

capstone

©2008, 2016 Heinemann Library
an imprint of Capstone Global Library, LLC. Chicago, Illinois

To contact Capstone Global Library, please
call 800-747-4992, or visit our web site
www.capstonepub.com

Designed by Kimberly R. Miracle and Betsy Wernert
Photo Research by Tracy Cummins and Heather Mauldin
Maps provided by Map Specialists

**Library of Congress Cataloging-in-Publication Data
is available on the Library of Congress website.**
    ISBN 978-1-4846-3688-6 (revised paperback)
    ISBN 978-1-4846-3494-3 (ebook)

Photo Credits

The author and publishers are grateful to the following for permission to reproduce copyright material: Alamy: Globe Photos/ZUMAPRESS.com, 16, Glow Images, 4; Capstone Press: Map Specialist, 29; Corbis: Royalty-Free, 20; Flickr: Official White House Photo, 18, Official White House Photo by Pete Souza, 10; Getty Images: Andrew Harrer/Bloomberg, 17, Douglas Graham/CQ Roll Call, 15, Hank Walker/The LIFE Picture Collection, 25, Jay L. Clendenin, 12, TIM SLOAN/AF, 8, Time Life Pictures/White House, 9; iStockphoto: Pgiam, 14, Rich Legg, 21; Shutterstock: Andrea Izzotti, 13, bikeriderlondon, 22, Drop of Light, 26, Jose Gil, 5, Joseph Sohm, 6, Konstantin L, 19, mdgn, 24, Monkey Business Images, 27, Orhan Cam, Cover; Thinkstock: Stockbyte, 23

Cover photograph reproduced with permission of AP Photo/Ron Edmonds.

Every effort has been made to contact copyright holders of any material reproduced in this book. Any omissions will be rectified in subsequent printings if notice is given to the publisher.

Table of Contents

Some words are shown in bold, **like this**. You can find out what they mean by looking in the glossary.

What Is Government?

The United States **federal government** runs the entire country. It is a **democracy**. This means it is made up of people who are **elected** (chosen) to run the country.

★ The United States federal government is in Washington, D.C.

Many people work in the federal government.
They work for all the **citizens** of the United States.

★
★ Barack Obama is talking with U.S. citizens.
★ He works in the federal government.

★ Citizens vote to choose their government leaders.

Citizens are people who live and vote in the United States. They vote to **elect** (choose) leaders in the government.

The government is made up of three branches (parts). Each part has a special job. The three branches of the **federal government** are the:

- **executive branch**
- **legislative branch**
- **judicial branch**.

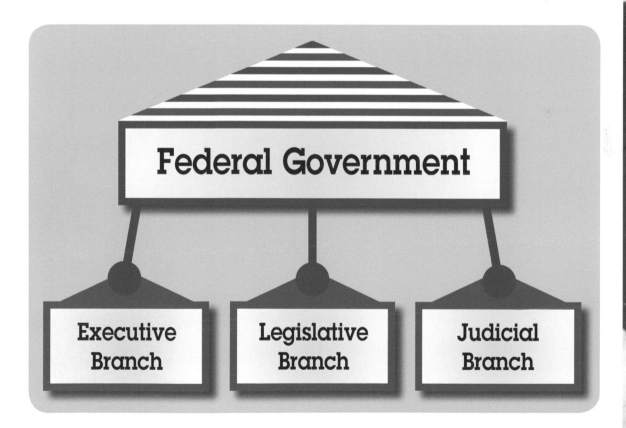

Federal Government

Executive Branch

Legislative Branch

Judicial Branch

The Executive Branch

The job of the **executive branch** is to make sure the laws are followed. Laws are rules that people must obey. Laws are made to help run the country for the good of everyone.

★★★ People who work in the executive branch meet to discuss how to run the country.

The main people who work in the executive branch are:

- the president of the United States
- the vice president of the United States
- the **Cabinet**.

★★★ The president meets with the Cabinet in the Cabinet room.

The president of the United States is the leader of the **executive branch**. The president makes sure the laws are being followed.

★★★★ The president reviews information from different members of the government.

The executive branch is divided into different departments (groups). The leader of each department is called a **secretary**. The **Cabinet** is made up of all the department secretaries.

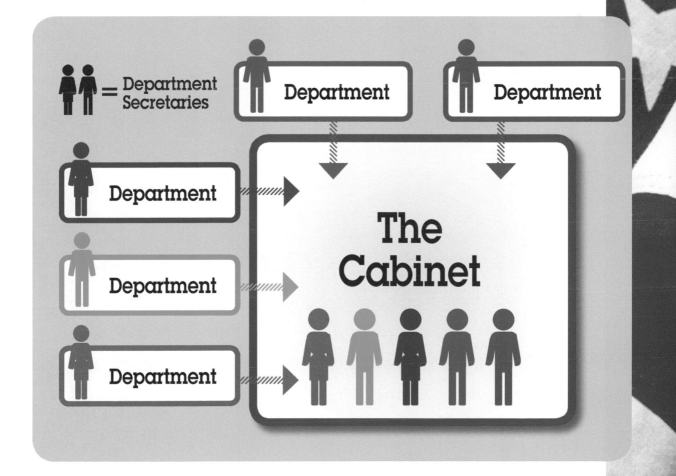

The secretary of education is meeting with President Bush at a school.

People who work in the **Cabinet** give advice to the president. For example, one **secretary** is from the Department of Education. She tells the president how schools and education may be improved.

★ The president lives and works in the White House.

People in the **executive branch** work in the White House. The White House is in Washington, D.C.

The Legislative Branch

Senate

House of Representatives

★★★ The two houses of Congress meet in the same building.

The **legislative branch** is the part of the government that makes laws. People in the legislative branch work in **Congress**. Congress is made of two houses, or groups.

The two houses of Congress are the **Senate** and the **House of Representatives**. People who work in the Senate are called senators. People who work in the House of Representatives are called representatives.

★★★ Senators and representatives work together on important issues.

★ This is the room where the Senate meets.

Each state is represented in the **Senate** and **House of Representatives**. All members of **Congress** are **elected** (chosen) by the American people.

Making Laws

Either house of Congress can propose (suggest) an idea for a new law. This idea is called a **bill**. One house of Congress looks at the bill to decide if it should become a law. If they vote in favor of the bill, it is sent to the other house.

★ Senators meet together to discuss new bills.

The other house of **Congress** reviews the **bill** to decide if it should become a law. If most people vote for the bill, it is sent to the president of the United States. If the president signs the bill, it becomes a law.

★ President Obama is signing a bill. It will become a new law.

★ This is the United States Capitol building.

Members of Congress work in the Capitol building.
The Capitol building is in Washington, D.C.

The Judicial Branch

People who work in the **judicial branch** make sure the laws are understood. They also decide if a law has been broken.

★ Judges must decide if a person or group has broken a law.

The main people who work in the judicial branch are **judges** and **lawyers**.

lawyer

judge

A **judge** is a person who makes decisions about whether a law has been broken. Judges work in **courts**. A court is a place people can go to if they feel a law has been broken.

A **lawyer** is a person who knows the laws. Lawyers help people who go to court. They talk to the judge for the person. They try to get the judge to agree with that person's opinion.

★★★ In some cases, a group of **citizens** decides if a law has been broken.

The Supreme Court

There are many **courts** in the **judicial branch**. The **Supreme Court** is the highest court in the judicial branch. It is in Washington, D.C.

★ This is the United States Supreme Court.

There are nine **judges** who work in the Supreme Court. Supreme Court judges are first chosen by the president of the United States. People in the **Senate** then vote to decide if they agree with the president's choice.

★★★ Thurgood Marshall was the first African-American judge to serve on the Supreme Court.

Working Together

★ People in the government work together to lead the country.

The three branches of government work together. While they each have a certain job, they must agree with the decisions of the other branches. One branch cannot make decisions for the entire country.

Each branch of government plays an important role in
running the United States of America.

Visiting the Capital of the United States

Washington D.C. is the capital of the United States. All three branches of government are located there. Below is a map of downtown Washington, D.C. It shows the location of some government buildings, museums, and monuments.

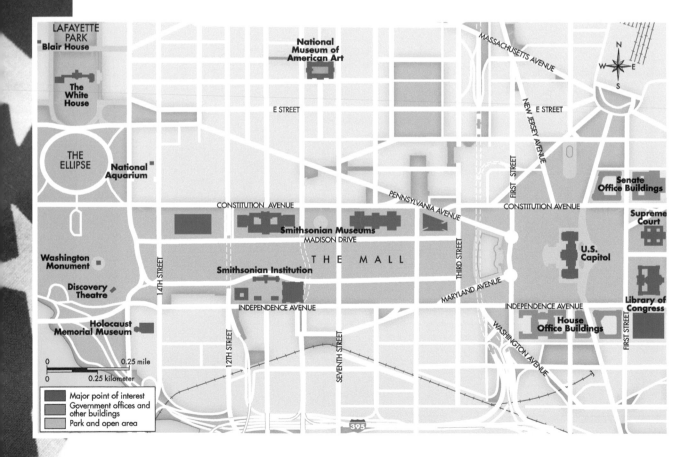

Government Fast Facts

★ A senator or representative is also called a congressman or congresswoman.

★ The **Cabinet** was created by George Washington, the first president of the United States.

★ The Capitol building is where people in the legislative branch meet together. The spelling of the Capitol building is with an "o."

★ A capital is the city where the government of a state or country is located. The spelling of "capital" is with an "a."

★ Washington, D.C. is not a state. It is called a territory.

Glossary

bill written proposal or idea for a new law

Cabinet group made up of all the department secretaries in the executive branch

citizen person who is born in the United States. People who have moved to the United States from another country can become citizens by taking a test.

Congress part of the government that makes laws

court place people can go if they feel a law has been broken

democracy country that is run by leaders who are elected (chosen) by the people in the country

elect choose a leader by voting

executive branch part of the United States federal government. This branch makes sure the laws in the United States are followed.

federal government group of leaders who run the entire country. In a federal government, the country is made up of many states.

House of Representatives house (group) in Congress where representatives from each state work

judge person who decides if a law has been understood or if it has been broken

judicial branch part of the United States federal government. This branch makes sure the laws (rules) in the country are understood.

lawyer person who knows the law. Lawyers help people who go to court.

legislative branch part of the United States federal government that makes laws

secretary leader of each department in the executive branch

Senate house (group) in Congress where two senators from each state work. Congress is where laws are made.

Supreme Court most powerful court in the United States government. It is part of the judicial branch.

More Books to Read

Catrow, David. *We the Kids*. New York: Penguin Young Readers, 2005.

Maestro, Betsy. *A More Perfect Union: The Story of Our Constitution*. New York: Harper Trophy, 1990.

Riehecky, Janet. *Citizenship*. Mankato, MN: Capstone Press, 2005.

Internet Sites

FactHound offers a safe, fun way to find Internet sites related to this book. All of the sites on FactHound have been researched by our staff

Visit www.fachound.com

Index